HIS GLORY

EXPERIENCE THE TRANSFORMING POWER OF GOD'S PRESENCE

VICTORIA OLADIPUPO

HIS GLORY

Copyright © 2019 by Victoria Oladipupo

Publishing Name
PVM Publishing

Website
www.pastorvictoria.org

First Edition
ISBN-13: 978-1-9161750-0-6- E-book
ISBN-13: 978-1-9161750-1-3- Paperback

Printed in the United Kingdom and the United States of America

Unless otherwise stated, all scripture quotes are taken from the King James Version; with emphasis added or paraphrased.

Publishing Consultants
Vike Springs Publishing Ltd.
www.vikesprings.com

For further information or contact Pastor Victoria please send an email to: pastorvictoria@ymail.com
Pastor Victoria's books are available at special discounts when purchased in bulk for promotions or as donations for educational, inspirational and training purposes.

LIMIT OF LIABILITY/ DISCLAIMER OF WARRANTY

This publication is designed to provide accurate and authoritative information in regard to the subject matter covered. It is sold with the understanding that the publisher and author are not engaged in rendering physiological, financial, legal or other licensed services. The publisher and the author make no representations or warranties with respect to the completeness of the contents of this work. If expert assistance or counselling is needed, the services of a specific professional should be sought. Neither the publisher nor the author shall be liable for damages arising here from. The fact that an organization or website is referred to in this work as a citation and/or a potential source of further information does not mean that the author or the publisher endorses the information that the organization or website may provide or recommendations it may make, nor does the cited organization endorse affiliation of any sort to this publication. Also, readers should be aware that due to the ever-changing information from the web, Internet websites and URLs listed in this work may have changed or been removed. All trademarks or names referenced in this book are the property of their respective owners, and the publisher and author are not associated with any product or vendor mentioned.

DEDICATION AND ACKNOWLEDGEMENTS

I dedicate this book to my mother, who is my role model, inspiration and the one who equipped me to do what I do best. I love and miss you every day.

I want to thank God, who made the completion of this book possible after many challenges. I want to thank everyone who encouraged, prayed for and helped me one way or another throughout this process. I want to thank my family and my children for supporting me continuously.

To God be the glory.

FOREWORD

My heart's desire is that every reader of this book experiences a prophetic dimension of glory. May it communicate a courageous thirst that will propel every reader into their divine glory by the help of the Holy Spirit's interpretation, in Jesus' Name. Amen!

CONTENTS

INTRODUCTION 1

CHAPTER ONE

PRECEDENCE OF GLORY 9

CHAPTER TWO

CARRIERS OF HIS GLORY 19

CHAPTER THREE

GATES OF GLORY 35

CHAPTER FOUR

FIGHT FOR YOUR FUTURE 45

CHAPTER FIVE

PRINCIPLES OF FASTING AND PRAYER .. 59

CHAPTER SIX

SET TIME FOR GLORY 67

INTRODUCTION

"When I consider thy heavens, the work of thy fingers, the moon and the stars, which thou hast ordained; what is man, that thou art mindful of him? And the son of man, that thou visitest him? For thou hast made him a little lower than the angels, and hast crowned him with glory and honour. Thou madest him to have dominion over the works of thy hands; thou hast put all things under his feet: All sheep and oxen, yea, and the beasts of the field; the fowl of the air, and the fish of the sea, and whatsoever passeth through the paths of the seas." Psalm 8:3-8

Kabod: The glory of God - His beauty, His splendour, His magnificence, His wealth and His honour can be experienced on earth as it is in heaven. That is our purpose on earth.

Glory was part of the composition of man at creation. The Psalmist was curious about how man is so different from other creatures that he has a special place in the heart of God, knowing full well that man is MORTAL. So how could an IMMORTAL BEING (God) care so much about MORTAL MAN?

An individual had to exhibit specific characteristics to be visited by the king. For there to be an individual on King David's mind, that person must have had something tangible to contribute to him or the kingdom he ruled over. A good example is the president of the United States of

America paying a visit to a man in a remote area in Somalia, openly expressing his intentions to treat this man carefully, or his desire to visit the man solely to see how he is faring. If something like this were to happen, one might conclude that there is something spectacular about the man in Somalia that nobody else knows. In this example, even the president of Somalia would be wondering what could make an American president bypass him to visit who many may refer to as a 'nobody' in his country.

This was the position of David when he wrote this passage. He knew man was created to be lower than the angels, but man is not required to worship angels (Rev. 19:10). God does not need to visit angels because they are with Him in His abode, but for man, God engaged on a journey, as God did with Adam (Gen. 3:8-10). This happened because God crowned man with glory and dominion over all creation (Gen. 1:26).

---

*Brethren, glory sets you apart
to enjoy preferential treatment.*

Glory attracts rank and favour to you: your location and qualifications are inconsequential when it is at work in your life. The Bible states that man took charge over all other creations because he had been crowned with glory (Gen. 1:26). God sets all other creatures under his feet

(Gen. 1:28). That is why it is an aberration for a Christian to believe the norm that he evolved from apes. All these animals were under man (Gen. 1:26). It was the glory that subjected them under man. The glory differentiated man from animals. Don't forget; the glory was a crown on man's head (John 19:9). The glory gave man dominion and a better reasoning faculty compared to animals. King Nebuchadnezzar is an example (Dan. 4:28-37).

When man fell in the Garden of Eden, the glory was lost (Gen. 3:1-24). The serpent became the instrument the devil used. So, the glory upon man was lost (Rom. 3:23). God then used the coat of skin from an animal to cover the nakedness of man (Gen. 3:21). Right then, from the Garden of Eden, the animals became more significant in their purpose because man lost his glory (Gen. 3:24). Man then needed the blood of the animals to cover his sins temporarily as atonement (Exodus 29:10-14; Num. 6:10-11).

This went on as the blood of animals was used for atonement, purification and acceptance offerings (Num. 29:11) throughout the Old Testament until the revelation of Jesus in the New Testament.

"And Joseph also went up from Galilee, out of the city of Nazareth, into Judaea, unto the city of David, which is called Bethlehem; (because he was of the house and lineage of David) To be taxed with Mary his

espoused wife, being great with child. And so it was, that, while they were there, the days were accomplished that she should be delivered. And she brought forth her firstborn son, and wrapped him in swaddling clothes, and laid him in a manger; because there was no room for them in the inn. And there were in the same country shepherds abiding in the field, keeping watch over their flock by night. And, lo, the angel of the Lord came upon them, and the glory of the Lord shone round about them: and they were sore afraid. And the angel said unto them, Fear not: for, behold, I bring you good tidings of great joy, which shall be to all people. For unto you is born this day in the city of David a Saviour, which is Christ the Lord. And this shall be a sign unto you; Ye shall find the babe wrapped in swaddling clothes, lying in a manger." Luke 2:4-12

God is a master planner. There is no situation He cannot manage for His glory.

Anything you can point to now as discomfort is to lead you into your glory. Time and chance are in His hand (Dan. 2:21).

Why was there a census at that time? Why was the delivery of Jesus about that time? Why was the inn filled up with people? Why was it that the one place available was in the manger? Why were the shepherds the first set of people to receive the good news of the birth of Jesus? Why was "seeing the child in the manger" the only sign given to the shepherds to recognise Jesus?

Jesus was born in the manger to take back the glory and restore it unto man (Luke 2:9; John 17:22). Don't forget; the main purpose of Jesus was to die for our sins so that His blood could be used for the eternal remission of our sins (Col. 1:20; Heb. 9:14). Before the death of Jesus on the cross of Calvary, the animals were fulfilling this mission temporarily. Therefore, Jesus went to the manger to tell the animals the perfect sacrifice for sin has come, and the lost glory was bequeathed back to Him (Luke 2:11-14).

Immediately after Jesus was born, the angel of the Lord went to meet the shepherds where they were watching the flocks by night (Luke 2:10). But why were they watching the flocks by night? For from the beginning it wasn't so. Arguably, it means there must be something about the sheep for them to be watched over by night.

The reason the angel went to the shepherds was to give them first-hand information that the tides were changing, that the glory that was lost would be restored to them and they would find the child in the manger.

Jesus became the brightness of God's glory and was raised above angels and other things in heaven, under heaven and beneath the earth. So, the hope of glory has been restored to man. Every man on earth now can claim his or her glory in Christ.

"Who being the brightness of his glory, and the express image of his person, and upholding all things by the word of his power, when he had by himself purged our sins, sat down on the right hand of the Majesty on high: Being made so much better than the angels, as he hath by inheritance obtained a more excellent name than they. For unto which of the angels said he at any time, Thou art my Son, this day have I begotten thee? And again, I will be to him a Father, and he shall be to me a Son? And again, when he bringeth in the first begotten into the world, he saith, and let all the angels of God worship him. And of the

angels he saith, Who maketh his angels spirits, and his ministers a flame of fire." Heb.1:3-7

"To them God willed to make known what are the riches of the glory of this mystery among the Gentiles: which is Christ in you, the hope of glory." Colossians 1:27 (NKJV)

Man now has a fresh glory he can lay claim on in Christ Jesus (Psalm 3:3, Job 29:20).

Beloved, here in this book is in-depth knowledge, tested scriptural principles and prayers that will launch you into HIS GLORY for your life, marriage, career, academics and ministry and in your health.

See you in GLORY.

CHAPTER ONE
PRECEDENCE OF GLORY

"*Arise, shine; For your light has come! And the glory of the LORD is risen upon you. For behold, the darkness shall cover the earth, And deep darkness the people; But the LORD will arise over you, And His glory will be seen upon you. The Gentiles shall come to your light, And kings to the brightness of your rising.*" Isaiah 60:1-3

There is always precedence to glory, and that is light. When the scripture says "arise, shine," it means man is a luminous being. And by luminous, I mean something with the ability to radiate light, brightness. In other words, it means something full of light because light is described as the symbol of knowledge, understanding and deep revelation about something. Daniel was said to have light in him (Daniel 5:8-12).

---

*Glory does not come on emptiness.
It is the knowledge of something, the
awareness of a particular deep
secret that provokes glory.*

According to the law of First Mention in theology, the word glory first appeared in Genesis 31:1. Looking at the content and context of it, we can trace what was called glory to all the healthy animals bequeathed to Jacob when he acted on the revelation the angel showed him in Genesis 31:6-12.

There is a level of light you need to get revealed. The first light we saw at creation when God said let there be light was not the light of the sun, moon or stars, but the light of **revelation** to make everything come bare. That light made the work of creation easy and fast. You too can be so full of light that your shining becomes easy. Knowledge is power! The reason you must seek light is that darkness has covered the earth and its people (Isaiah 60:2). Since the prophecy has been fulfilled, the solution must be fulfilled too in your life. Your light must come in Jesus' name. Amen!

You must have a revelation of who God has created you to be. It is this light that will be the stamina for the glory to be revealed in you. Going by the scripture, "The glory of the Lord is risen upon you." The word "risen", in Hebrew – 'za rach' means climb, so you need the stamina to be able to carry the glory and to carry it for a long duration of time because the glory is weighty.

The stamina you need for the sustenance of enduring glory is the revelation of whom God is.

Glory is the Lord Himself arising upon you.

Are you sure you won't crash acting as a platform for God to stand on? The first point of call is to, therefore, seek the light.

When you've received the light, shining is non-negotiable.

Full knowledge of who you are is the platform for your rising - not just head knowledge but an experiential knowledge that has filled your subconscious, which in turn affects your daily activities.

It is in the DNA of light to shine. It is when you have this kind of light that you shine effortlessly. This light (knowledge) is what makes you luminous because you contracted the light from the Father of Lights (James 1:27).

The same way light attracts, knowledge also attracts. Knowledge attracts glory. Knowledge breaks the backbone of servitude. Jacob would have died a pauper in the house of Laban, except for the light, the in-depth knowledge revealed to him. Before he got the knowledge, Laban had changed his wages ten times, and that could have continued if not for the light that broke the evil trend.

---

*If you have noticed any sinister
trend in your life and you desire
glory in that area, go and seek
light and knowledge in that area.*

Servitude, shame, lack, sickness, barrenness all have their strength in ignorance. Wisdom enriches, knowledge liberates and understanding gives posterity.

---

*The end of every man with eternal
light or knowledge is glory.*

---

*"And **we know** that all things work together for good for those who love God, to those who are **the called** according to His purpose. For whom He **foreknew**, He also predestined to be conformed to the*

*image of His son, that He might be the firstborn among many brethren. Moreover, whom He **predestined**, these He also **called**; whom He called, these He also **justified**; and whom He justified, these He also **glorified.***" (Romans 8:28-30)

The knowledge of every man who must end in glory must be in these four areas:

Foreknew: You must know God's intent behind your birth. You must seek to know the prophetic word hanging over your life.

Pre-destined: God had concluded your destination before you got here, so seek to know the destination He has concluded for you. God concluded your destination, but the pathway is still under construction.

Called: Know what He has called you to do. Know your purpose. Know what to do to get to the destination He has concluded. Romans 8:28b says "to those who are **THE CALLED** according to His purpose," not who are called.

Your calling is not in the future.
It was concluded before you came.

So, you are part of THE CALLED already. Find it out!

Justified: You must know what He has freely given you as a result of the finished work of Christ. You must know and understand the benefits of your position in Christ Jesus.

Another important precedence to glory is grace. Grace is God's ability to help a man despite his frailty, limitations and shortcomings.

"For the Lord God is a sun and shield, the Lord will give grace and glory: no good thing will He withhold from those who walk uprightly." Psalm 84:11

Both grace and glory are gifts from God. You do not get them by your labour. They are God's gifts, and God Himself administers the gifts.

---

*Glory is hard to come by when
grace has not been released.*

Grace does the work of addition, and what He adds is glory.

"And Moses said to the Lord, see, thou sayest unto me, bring up this people: and thou hast not let me know whom thou wilt send with me. Yet thou hast said, I know thee by name, and thou hast also found grace in my sight. Now therefore, I pray thee, if I have found grace in your sight, shew me now thy way, that I may know thee and that I may find grace in thy sight. And consider that this nation is thy people. And He said, my presence will go with thee, and I will give thee rest. And he said unto Him, if thy presence go not with us, carry us not up hence. For wherein shall it be known here that I and thy people have found grace in thy sight? Is it not in that thou goes with us? So shall we be separated, I and thy people, from all the people that are upon the face of the earth. And the Lord said unto Moses, I will do this thing also that thou hast spoken: for thou has found grace in my sight and I know thee by name. And he said, I beseech thee, shew me thy glory." Exodus 33:12-18

---

*Grace has levels and depths. The product
of grace is always magnificent, regardless
of the level you possess. Grace does not
leave any man the way he met them;
it transforms the lives of its recipients.*

The difference between man and his glorious future is GRACE. The end product of grace is GLORY.

Moses was communing with God regarding the assignment before him, and immediately after God revealed to him that he had found grace in his sight, the tone of the conversation changed. Moses received the confidence to ask for what he wouldn't have been bold to ask for initially.

---

*Grace imparts boldness and
confidence into the heart of a man.*

It makes you ask in the capacity of God, not in what you think you're worth.

"Let us therefore come boldly unto the throne of grace, that we may obtain mercy and find grace to help in time of need." Hebrews 4:16

Brethren, you need grace to muster enough confidence to ask for what you need when in the presence of who could help. The fear of not being granted what you ask for might make you ask amiss.

When grace is available, everything is possible.

No man can resist the grace upon you - even God himself would not because He is a gracious God. Moses began to ask for some deep and great things and God put it this way - "I will do this thing also which thou hast spoken." This suggests to me that Moses's requests were not in God's primary agenda for him, but because he asked, it was done. Moses went further by asking God to show him His glory, and that was the deal breaker. God said 'I will make provision for this hard thing you asked also, although no man sees me and still lives but for you, I will hide you in a place beside me in the clift of the rock' (Exodus 33:19-23).

Grace is God's partiality in fairness. What would you call it when God said "Jacob have I loved, Esau have I hated," even before both were born? Is there unrighteousness with God? God forbid.

*When you see a man with grace, it will
be as if God is partial. Grace makes
all the difference in life.*

Just like the story of the prodigal son; the elder brother thought their father was partial by celebrating his younger brother who had squandered the resources of the father, but that was grace and mercy in display (Luke 15:11-32).

Grace always restores to the original state with all the benefits included, even if you may have lost them before. Through grace, God makes provision for your request. Don't forget; Psalm 84:11 tells us no good thing will be withheld. It is thus an aberration for any man to keep quiet when you know grace is available. You can only plunder the enemies in the season of grace.

No matter what is happening in your country, around you or to the people who are to help you, no good thing will be withheld from you this season in Jesus' name. The Israelites plundered the Egyptians at the time they were mourning, yet they couldn't withhold what they asked from them (Exodus 13:31-36).

CHAPTER TWO
CARRIERS OF HIS GLORY

"*Arise, shine; For your light has come! And the glory of the LORD is risen upon you. For behold, the darkness shall cover the earth, And deep darkness the people; But the LORD will arise over you, And His glory will be seen upon you. The Gentiles shall come to your light, and kings to the brightness of your rising.*" Isaiah 60:1-3

God gave us the charge to 'arise and shine'. He also gave two compelling reasons why: first, the positive reason – 'your light has come, and the glory of the Lord is risen upon you', but also the negative reason – 'darkness will cover the earth, and deep darkness will cover the people'.

But rise up! Why? The glory of God has risen over you.

When I say I'm a glory carrier, what exactly do I mean? What does it mean to carry the glory of God?

The word glory is the Hebrew word *'kabod'*, which means weight, weightiness, splendour, wealth, magnificence or honour. By definition, the word 'glory' is very simple:

The glory of God is the tangible manifestation of the presence of God.

The glory of God is the splendour of God.

The glory of God is the majesty, the weightiness, the resplendence, the magnificence, the wealth and the honour of God.

The glory of God is something that can be experienced. When you encounter a person who is carrying the glory of God, you know it. You can feel it, and sometimes you can see it. To carry means to transport or conduct from one place to another.

The glory of God distinguishes you; it makes you attractive and magnetic, and it is a trigger for favour.

When you carry the glory of God, you command such a powerful magnetic force that nations are attracted to you, so much that they begin to move towards your light. Isaiah 60:3 says 'The Gentiles shall come to your light, and kings to the brightness of your rising.' Now when we say kings, notice we are not just talking about the Queen or King in Monarch. The word 'kings' also refers to heads of corporations and CEOs. People in high places will be attracted to the glory that is upon you.

The day is coming when all the majestic powers of this world will come and bask in the light of the glory of God's people.

God can choose someone to be the carrier of His glory, and I pray that God shall make you the carrier of His glory in Jesus' name. Amen!

God's glory does not just show up anywhere, anytime or anyhow. God is very selective about where He places His glory, and He has chosen to place His glory upon you, His covenant child. So, here's the deal - if you do not carry the glory of God, His glory will not be seen because the glory of God does not operate in a vacuum - there must be a carrier. The Lord shall make your house the carrier of His glory in Jesus' name.

Embrace your office as a glory carrier because you are the only hope that the world has.

If you do not carry the glory, the glory cannot be seen. If you do not shine your light, the world is doomed to dwell in darkness.

Isaiah 60:2 says 'For behold, the darkness shall cover the earth, and deep darkness the people.'

We were created in the image of God to be glory carriers.

"For God, who commanded the light to shine out of darkness has shined in our hearts, to give the light of the knowledge of the glory of God in the face of Jesus Christ but we have this treasure in earthen vessels, that the excellency of power may be of God, and not us." II Corinthians 4:6-7

God has glory but seeks to put this glory on man so that man could return the glory back to Him. Clay has no glory, but God beautifies the clay to show how wondrous His acts are, and in the quest, man will recognise Him as the source and return the glory back to Him.

THE ESSENCE OF GLORY

When God puts His glory on a man or shows forth His glory in the life of a man, it is for some reasons like:

Confirmation:

Glory is to confirm God's presence with a man.

It reveals God's election when there is contest or rivalry as the case may be. So, God uses glory to silence the enemies and to approve His elected. Aaron and Hannah are case studies.

Beauty:

The beauty of life is glory. Glory helps a man to forget the miseries of past years. It turns your scars to beauty. It turns your pain to gain. Glory beautifies life.

Sanctification:

Contrary to the belief of many, glory calls you to a life of sanctity. It shuns profaned lifestyles. A man who wants to see God's glory must live a separated life unto God (Exodus 3:1-5).

KINDS OF GLORY

"All flesh is not the same flesh, but there is one kind of flesh of men, another flesh of animals, another of fish, and another of birds. There are also celestial bodies and terrestrial bodies; but the glory of the celestial is one, and the glory of the terrestrial is another. There is one glory of the sun, another glory of the moon, and another glory of the stars; for one star differs from another star in glory." I Corinthians 15:39-41

Glory is in levels and stages. Every human represents a star. So, as stars differ from stars in nature or size, so also are they in glory. In the same vein, every human has glory but not in the same quantum.

It is the measure of the darkness
around us that determines the kind
of star we are because the illumination
from the star must be able to dispel
the darkness around us.

The light is not for fun; neither is the glory for play. Glory does not compete just as stars don't compete. Instead, they complement each other in the sky. It is important we understand this so that our lives won't be a breeding ground for pride and jealousy.

---

*Great glory is a product of a
great problem solved or great
darkness dispelled.*

We all have celestial glory, but not all celestial glory has been downloaded to terrestrial glory. It is a life of frustration when all you can point to is celestial glory, the spiritual blessing or promises God has given without them manifesting in the terrestrial world. Even Jesus had to pray for the manifestation of the celestial glory in the terrestrial world. We need both to fully showcase His glory in our lives.

"Jesus spoke these words, lifted up His eyes to heaven, and said: Father, the hour has come. Glorify Your Son, that Your Son also may glorify You, as You have given Him authority over all flesh, that He should give eternal life to as many as You have given Him. And this is eternal life, that they may know You, the only true God, and Jesus Christ whom You have sent. I have glorified You on the earth. I have finished the work which You have given Me to do. And now, O Father, glorify Me together with Yourself, with the glory which I had with You before the world was." John 17:1-5

Brethren, you need terrestrial glory for you to maximise your destiny fully. This is where the devil and his demons are dealing with the human race in hindering the celestial glory from manifesting in the terrestrial world, and this explains the reason we have the following kinds of glory:

1. Dumb Glory
2. Speaking Glory
3. Sleeping Glory
4. Awaked Glory

DUMB GLORY: Glory is meant to speak. When glory remains in the celestial realm without any terrestrial manifestation, such glory is said to be dumb. Hence, gentiles, kings and queens can't come to its brightness; neither does it bring praises to God.

"Now there was found in it a poor wise man, and he by his wisdom delivered the city; yet no man remembered that same poor man. Then said I, wisdom is better than strength: nevertheless the poor man's wisdom is despised, and his words are not heard. The words of a wise men are heard in quiet, more than the cry of him that ruleth among fools." Eccl. 9:15-17

SPEAKING GLORY: When there is an expression or manifestation of the celestial glory in the terrestrial world, glory, in this case, is speaking.

"To the end that my glory may sing praise to you and not be silent. O LORD my God, I will give thanks to You forever." Psalms 30:12

"The heavens declare the glory of God; And the firmament shows His handiwork. Day unto day utters speech, And night unto night reveals knowledge. There is no speech nor language Where their voice is not heard. Their line has gone out through all the earth, And their words to the end of the world. In them He has set a tabernacle for the sun." Psalms 19:1-4

SLEEPING GLORY: This is glory that has gone into oblivion after some periods of shining. The celestial glory was being expressed in the terrestrial at a time but no longer does so. The glory has become inactive or numb. This is what happens to a man or business that was thriving but is not anymore. At this time of inactiveness, the glory can't attract benefactors or anything good to the man or establishment.

---

*Glory has no day or night; it's meant
to be active and shining at all times.*

God never sleeps nor slumbers, and since He is the king of glory, glory neither sleeps nor slumbers (Psalms 121:4).

AWAKED GLORY: This is a restored glory. A glory that was cut off before from shining but is now back to shining in the terrestrial.

"Awake, my glory! Awake, lute and harp! I will awaken the dawn." Psalms 57:8

Glory is the guiding light that connects your benefactor to where you are. No good thing can be diverted when your glory is actively shining (Matthew 2:9-11).

PROTECTION OVER THE GLORY

The devil has three missions, which are to steal, to kill and to destroy (John 10:10). This is perpetuated in the dark. Darkness is the breeding ground for the works of the devil. No thief operates in the presence of floodlight, so to achieve their purpose, they have to deal with the light first. And if the light (knowledge, direction) in you, as we have shared in the first chapter of this book, is intact, no devil can attack your glory.

Jesus and Moses were preserved from the onslaught of destiny in their days based on the light of direction from birth.

"And the Lord will create upon every dwelling place of mount Zion, and upon her assemblies, a cloud and smoke by day, and the shining of a flaming fire by night for upon ALL the GLORY shall be a DEFENCE." Isaiah 4:5

ACCESSING HIS GLORY

To access the glory or to translate the celestial glory into the terrestrial world, the following should be done:

Christ in You: The King of Glory must be in you. He must be formed in you.

It's not enough to be in Christ;
Christ must also be in you.

A child or a babe in God cannot access glory. Paul was speaking in Galatians 4 about how an heir who is a child can't access what the father has unless she grows up. He can only grow up when Christ is formed in him.

"My little children, of whom I travail in birth again until Christ be formed in you." Galatians 4:19

"To whom God would make known what is the riches of the glory of this mystery among the gentiles; which is Christ in you, the hope of glory." Colossians. 1:27

Deal with Uzziah: I pray this a lot with my prayer team. Uzziah was a great king who grew so mighty through several inventions, conquered territories. He ruled Judah for fifty-two years, and there was virtually nothing he didn't accomplish as a man and a King. God helped him so much that he was very great but thought, because God had helped him, he could also perform the duty of the priest in the temple. This became his waterloo. After he became a leper, he was still a figure of a god in the sight of the citizenry because of his level of achievement. That was the height of success Judah had seen - his influence was so mighty that even the vision of prophet Isaiah about God was clouded. God had another realm of glory he wanted to reveal to Judah, especially Isaiah in his prophetic ministry.

"In the year that King Uzziah died, I saw the Lord sitting on a throne, high and lifted up, and the train of His robe filled the temple. Above it stood seraphim; each one had six wings: with two he covered his face, with two he covered his feet, and with two he flew. And one cried to another and said: 'Holy, holy, holy is the LORD of hosts; The whole earth is full of His glory! '" Isaiah 6:1-3

What does Uzziah typify?
    i.   Past achievement
    ii. Pride
    iii. Addiction

Live the Word:

Let the word of God be your anchor in every situation.

Be a custodian of the word of truth. Fill your heart with it and meditate on it day and night (Joshua 1:8).

"And the Word was made flesh and dwelt among us, (and we beheld His glory, the glory as of the only begotten of the Father) full of grace and truth." (John 1:14)

Jesus carried the glory of God because when He walked the earth, He was the living manifestation of the word of God.

Whenever the word becomes flesh, the glory of God is revealed.

Do the Works: For every promise or word given, there is a work to be done. It is the agreement of humanity and divinity that produces the miraculous.

"Let your light so shine before men, that they may see your good works and glorify your Father in heaven." Matthew 5:16

Be ready to take a risk for the sake of God. Obed-Edom took risks to accept the ark of the covenant into his house for safe keeping.

In the book of Hebrews, chapter 11, the Bible provides a few examples of people who enjoyed the glory of God. All of these people have some characteristics in common, and we want to discuss a few of them.

1. **Abel**: The story of Abel can be found in Genesis 4 and Hebrews 11:4 where the Bible says that "by faith, Abel offered unto God a more excellent sacrifice than Cain and by which he obtained witness that he was righteous". Abel was a carrier of the glory of God because of his giving. Our giving can help us to enjoy the glory of God in such a dimension we have never seen before. Abel gave his substance sacrificially unto God, and his offering was accepted whereas Cain's offering was rejected because he gave less than his best.

2. **Enoch**: The story of Enoch can be found in Genesis 5:22 – 24 and in Hebrews 11:5 where the Bible says that "by faith Enoch was translated that he should not see death; and was not found, because God had translated him: for before his translation he had this testimony that he pleased

God". Enoch lived such a holy life, and God's glory was so much upon him that he was prevented from experiencing physical death.

3. **Noah**: The story of Noah can be found in Genesis 6 – 8 and in Hebrews 11:7 where the Bible says that "by faith Noah being warned of God of things not seen as yet, moved with fear, prepared an ark to the saving of his house; by which he condemned the world". Noah enjoyed the glory because he had the fear of God in him and obeyed God even though he did not fully understand God's instruction to him. Noah and his household were countercultural people, and when others were mocking him because of his obedience, Noah enjoyed the glory of God.

4. **Abraham**: The story of Abraham can be found in Genesis 12 and Hebrews 11:8 where the Bible says "by faith Abraham when he was called to go out into a place which he should afterwards receive for an inheritance, obeyed; and he went out not knowing whither he went". Obedience and faith made Abraham enjoy God's glory. If we determine in our hearts to honour God with our obedience and our faith, we will enjoy His glory as Abraham did.

5. **Isaac**: The story of Isaac can be found in Genesis 24:63; 25:21 and in Hebrews 11:20 where the Bible says that "by faith Isaac blessed Jacob and Esau concerning things to come". Isaac enjoyed the glory of God because he was a man

given to prayer. In Genesis 24:63, he was seen spending time alone with God and in Genesis 25:21, he prayed for Rebekah, his wife because she was barren, and God answered him.

6. Jacob: The story of Jacob can be found in Genesis 32 and Hebrews 11:21 where the Bible says that "by faith Jacob when he was dying blessed both the sons of Joseph and worshipped leaning upon the top of his staff". Jacob's thirst for more of God transformed his life, and he enjoyed a name change and the glory of God.

"O God, You are my God; Early will I seek You; My soul thirsts for You; My flesh longs for You In a dry and thirsty land where there is no water. So I have looked for You in the sanctuary, To see Your power and Your glory. Because Your lovingkindness is better than life, My lips shall praise You. Thus I will bless You while I live; I will lift up my hands in Your name. My soul shall be satisfied as with marrow and fatness, And my mouth shall praise You with joyful lips. When I remember You on my bed, I meditate on You in the night watches. Because You have been my help, Therefore in the shadow of Your wings I will rejoice. My soul follows close behind You; Your right hand upholds me. But those who seek my life, to destroy it, Shall go into the lower parts of the earth. They shall fall by the sword; They shall be a portion for jackals. But the king shall rejoice in God; Everyone who swears by Him shall glory; But the mouth of those who speak lies shall be stopped." Psalms 63:1-11

CHAPTER THREE
GATES OF GLORY

"Lift up your heads, O ye gates! And be lifted up, ye everlasting doors! And the King of glory shall come in. Who is this King of glory? The LORD strong and mighty, The LORD mighty in battle. Lift up your heads, O ye gates! Lift up, ye everlasting doors! And the King of glory shall come in. Who is this King of glory? The LORD of hosts, He is the King of glory."
Psalms 24:7-10

To you reading this book, whose gates have been locked, whose doors have been barricaded, they shall be opened in Jesus' name.

It doesn't matter if the doors are shut, locked and guarded. God has provided you with keys and a divine grace that will allow you to pass through them (Robert Pace). And that's what I want to talk about next - how to open closed doors.

Gates and doors that lead to your place of glory, gates that lead to the top and the gates of your prosperity shall open this year in Jesus' name.

Miracles happen at the gates; ask the four lepers (II Kings 7:3-16)! Even the king was in the palace, and he did not have power over the economy, but the four lepers entered the gate of glory.

The gate is the place of decision, where the destiny of nations and her people is determined. When the prophetic word came, it came to the lepers at the gate.

Who is sitting at the gates of your breakthrough, saying the King of Glory will not come in? Who is sitting at the gate of your marriage? Who is sitting at the gate of your womb? I don't know what principalities are sitting at the neck of your womb called fibroid, saying the king of glory will not come in, but I'm here to prophesy that every gate that is barred shall be opened now in the name of Jesus. It shall be open today! It shall be opened this month!

Why are we talking about gates?

When Joshua defeated Jericho, one of the curses he placed was on the gate, saying whoever tried to build the gate again would build the foundation with his firstborn, and the day he completes it, he would set up its gates at the cost of his last born.

"Then Joshua charged them at that time, saying, 'Cursed be the man before the LORD who rises up and builds this city Jericho; he shall lay its foundation with his firstborn, and with his youngest he shall set up its gates.'" Joshua 6:26

"...and the gates of Hades shall not prevail against it." Matthew 16:18b

The Bible says the Proverbs 31 woman's husband sits at the gate, that he was announced at the gate.

Hear me; many Christians are praying for open doors while the gates are closed.

If your door is open and the gate is closed, nothing good can come in.

Your gates must be continually opened for glory to come in (Isaiah 60:11).

The gate to the billions in your business, the gate to your marriage shall open today. Any

Prince of Persia in charge of your gate shall be uprooted in the name of Jesus. On this Mount Zion, your gate of deliverance shall be opened in the name of Jesus (Obadiah 1:7).

"Oh, that men would praise the LORD for His goodness, And for His wonderful works to the children of men! For He has broken the gates of bronze, and cut the bars of iron in sunder." Psalms 107:15-16

When the gates are open, the glory of the Lord shall be revealed over your household.

Esther 6:2 lets us know the keeper of the gate is superior to the keeper of the door.

What enters through the gate can also come in through the door.

And Esther chapter 3 lets us know that the reason why Haman hated Mordecai is because he was at the gate - it is he who is at the gate that can give you entrance.

Haman knew that when he got to the gate, regardless of his high position, he would have to meet the Jewish man at the gate before he could meet the king.

Jericho's gate was powerfully shut, and nobody came in, and nobody went out. That is the power of a gate.

They did not want Joshua and the Israelites to enter, and the Bible says the Lord God gave Joshua a supernatural formula.

I decree today, to those of you who will believe, the Lord shall give you the secret code to the gate over your life in Jesus' name. Amen!

The Bible says they marched around the gate for seven days, and the wall sank, and the gate collapsed, so also, I decree that the walls that surround you shall come down in the name of Jesus. I declare your victory!

Hear me; when the gate is locked,
all you need is to use the divine
power of Jehovah.

Hammers cannot open it. To push the gate is a waste of effort. Joshua did not push the gate. You ought to stop struggling and sweating to open the gate by manipulation.

"Behold, children are a heritage from the LORD, The fruit of the womb is a reward. Like arrows in the hand of a warrior, So are the children of one's youth. Happy is the man who has his quiver full of them; They shall

not be ashamed, But shall speak with their enemies in the gate." Psalms 127:3-5

Jesus, being the son of God, has defeated the chief enemy, the devil at the gate. He fought the battle and won.

That means you must continue to pray for your children so they will not have to fight your battles at the gate. They are to destroy the enemy at their gate. Your children shall conquer their enemy at the gate in Jesus' name. Any enemy debarring them, obstructing them, today is destroyed at the gate.

Herod put a man of God, Peter by name, in a maximum prison and locked the gates in Acts 12:1-11, and the Bible said Peter was sleeping in the midst of soldiers.

I want to make something expressly clear: you need open doors! You can't live without them.

*If you are locked behind closed
doors, you are incarcerated!*

You are merely existing, not thriving. Prisons confine and prevent people from passing into places of freedom. That's why they're built with thick cement walls and cold steel doors.

*But know this: there is no door so
thick, none so strong, none so securely
locked that the Lord Almighty cannot
simply speak His Word and unhinge
before you! The power of Christ opens
doors that seem impenetrably shut!*

That is what Isaiah 45:1 means where it says, "[I will] open doors before you . . . I will shatter the doors of bronze and cut through their iron bars."

*When the sovereign Lord speaks, no
door can remain shut! The sole aim
of deliverance is for you to enjoy
the glory.*

If you are still struggling even after being delivered from the power of sin, it is because the gates to the city have not been opened unto you. Some gates lead to the city. When this kind of gate is shut, one can live his entire life in obscurity without enjoying any glory. You do not need the chains alone to fall off; you need the iron gates to the city to be opened too.

The iron gate was described as 'him'. Any power in the form of a gate that does not want you to enter the promised land shall die in the name of Jesus. Every human manipulation standing against your glory is frustrated in Jesus' name.

Queen Vashti's divorce was orchestrated by Menucans. Peter was about to be killed by a man called Herod.

Who is this gate standing against you, keeping you from entering the place of success? Who is this gate standing against the manifestation of your glory? Who is that strongman in your dream standing against your marriage? Who put you in this position where you are tied down? Who has locked you up? Who is controlling your spirit? Who is blocking your ministry? Who is standing against your progress? Who is that human agent raining curses and doing incantation on you? All these people are gates standing against your glory.

When Jesus was about to enter to deliver us, He said 'lift up your head oh ye gates'. Gates with heads signifies evil forces in human vessels. It continues to say that the gate answered and said 'who is this king of glory?' How can a gate talk?

Whatever has been speaking back to you, whatever has been contradicting your voice, whatever has been disturbing your prayer, they are demolished now in Jesus' name.

Just as the gate opens on its own accord, from now on gates shall be opened for you on their own accord.

That means from now on things will be easy for you. Where you have tried, it will be easy in Jesus' name. Where you have been insulted, you shall be celebrated. Where you have been rejected, you shall be needed. Where you have been refused, you shall be celebrated, in the name of God the Father, Son and the Holy Spirit. Amen!

CHAPTER FOUR
FIGHT FOR YOUR FUTURE

*"*A*nd I looked, and arose and said to the nobles, to the leaders, and to the rest of the people, 'Do not be afraid of them. Remember the Lord, great and awesome, and fight for your brethren, your sons, your daughters, your wives, and your houses.'"* Nehemiah 4:14

The fight for the future is NOW.

When you do not own your battle today, the future suffers. Some victories are generational, as well as some failures. When you do not handle some issues today, they spill over to tomorrow, and then they become more difficult.

Fight with the future in mind.

This was the admonition of Nehemiah to the people of Judah when Sanballat conspired with Tobiah, an Ammonite to fight against the rebuilding of the wall of Jerusalem. The wall of Jerusalem served as protection or security over everything Jerusalem stands for. So, the battle to rebuild the wall was a fierce one because it affected their economy, family, social life and much more.

There are some battles you win, and the victories last for generations. That means nobody in your lineage will be under such siege again. This was the situation of the Israelites under King Saul (I Sam. 17:25). All citizenries were under tributes. Nobody was free except the people of the king's household to whom the tribute was paid. The king can seize any of their lands, daughters, sons and wives as possessions without anyone questioning his actions. But the battle of who would fight the Philistine Goliath came up. One of the rewards King Saul promised to give to the person that fought Goliath was to make their father's house free in Israel. You don't know what that meant to an Israelite. It meant your family was free from taxes and tributes, and no king can take your possessions for himself again. Alas, the good thing is that not all family members will have to fight this battle for freedom. The battle must be fought by just one person. And such a person wouldn't only be fighting for himself or herself, but the burden to set the whole family free is on his or her shoulders. So, when David volunteered to fight, he was fighting for the household of Jesse to be free from bondage or tributes. He fought with the future in mind. He fought with his sons, daughters, brethren, wives and grandchildren in mind.

This chapter is to open your mind to know why you are fighting, waking you up to the responsibility hanging on your shoulders.

You must be sure of the reason you are fighting and what the outcome would be.

David asked the people what reward would be given to the person that fought with the Philistine. He needed the information to know what was at stake, whether he fought or not. Even Paul said in I Corinthians 9:26 'I therefore so run, not as uncertainty; so fight I not as one who beat the air'. Being clear of the intention and reward of a battle makes you focused and resilient on overcoming the battle (I Samuel 17:25-26).

"Then he stood and cried out to the armies of Israel, and said to them, 'Why have you come out to line up for battle? Am I not a Philistine, and you the servants of Saul? Choose a man for yourselves, and let him come down to me. If he is able to fight with me and kill

me, then we will be your servants. But if I prevail against him and kill him, then you shall be our servants and serve us.' And the Philistine said, 'I defy the armies of Israel this day; give me a man, that we may fight together.' When Saul and all Israel heard these words of the Philistine, they were dismayed and greatly afraid." I Sam. 17:8-11

You don't fight the battle of destiny by nomination but by choice.

Goliath had been calling on Saul to choose someone to represent them in the battle of life, but no! It doesn't work that way. Fighting a battle of life is a personal decision. For forty days, Saul could not nominate anyone, despite having several soldiers in his army, and he himself couldn't go and fight, even as the captain of the armies of Israel.

Nobody wanted to be responsible, and irresponsibility prolongs a battle. Indecision makes things tougher.

Thanks to God, somebody volunteered to step out of the norm. It was surprising the person was not a trained soldier but had a heart for responsibility.

*Glory always looks for the heart
that is ready to take responsibilities
to rest on.*

David took the responsibility to fight for a national honour. He took up the challenge of determining the destiny of a whole nation because Goliath had said whoever wins would subjugate the nation that loses as a servant.

"Be strong and quit yourself like men, O ye philistines that ye be not servants unto the Hebrews, as they have been to you: quit yourselves like men and fight." I Samuel 4:9

Quit yourself as a man, and fight for your future. Be responsible and fight. Decide to fight for your future. Fight for your marriage. Fight for your family. Fight for your relationship. Fight for your wife/husband. Fight for your children. Fight for your health. Fight for your job or business. Fight for your destiny, and fight for your church. Engage and fight. You need to fight to claim your lot, fight to keep your ground, fight to keep your land, fight to keep your position.

"And from the days of John the Baptist until now, the kingdom of Heaven suffereth violence and the violent take it by force." Matthew 11:12

Fight with your weapon. Fight with prayer, fight with revelation, fight with fasting, fight with the scripture. Your mouth, hands and fingers are made to fight (Psalms 144:1).

This fight is a good fight; you don't have to cower in fear.

He that is in you is greater. Know that this fight is a good fight because someone has fought and won the battle on your behalf. He only left you to claim the victory of the battle.

"Fight the good fight of faith, lay hold on eternal life, where unto thou art also called, and hast professed a good profession before many witness." I Timothy 6:12

"For whatsoever is born of God overcometh the world; and this is the victory that overcometh the world, even our faith." I John 5:4

When Jesus died on the cross and resurrected, He disposed the devil, our arch enemy of his power and made a public show of the victory. It is a known fact. The victory Jesus won was not done in the corner; it was open, and the devil can't deny it. So, all Christ did, He did on your behalf. When He said 'it is finished' on the cross, nothing was left to be done. The requirement for your deliverance and victory was a done deal. Jesus never needed the victory, but He possessed the victory for you. So, the question is, what is now left for me to do to enjoy this victory? Some will think giving your life to Jesus should exempt you from temptations and challenges. No, sir; it is to give you victory over the challenges of life.

"These things I have spoken unto you that in me you might have peace. In the world ye shall have tribulation, but be of good cheer; I have overcome the world." John 16:33

Everything Christ did for us, He did in advance, even before that situation surfaced. Do not forget He is omniscient. It is wonderful hearing Jesus making a futuristic statement like 'in the world you shall have tribulation', meaning the tribulation is yet to come, and then telling them He has overcome the tribulation. This is what we can't comprehend about the work Jesus did on the cross as a man. We cannot come to terms with the fact something would be done before our great-grandparents were born and we would be part of the provision. Some say if He had overcome the world, then our problems should not surface at all, and we should have problem-free lives, but that is not the way it has been fashioned. This pattern was to humiliate the devil of all his craftiness in painting the picture of an awful scary life for every individual. So, God created this pattern of you believing and exercising that knowledge in your situation to fix everything the devil thinks he is doing. This pattern is a faith pattern, and it has to do with your mind and your mouth. As a result, the battle we are to fight now is a battle of the mind with the weapon of the mouth. Every Christian is, therefore, in a fight of faith.

What is a fight of faith? It is insisting on God's provisions, till the redemptive work of Christ is experienced in your life irrespective of the present challenges. It is you insisting that what God has said concerning your situation will become a reality. The gateway to these realities is through your mind and your mouth.

"That if thou shalt confess with thy mouth the Lord Jesus, and shalt believe in thine heart that God hath raised him from the dead, thou shalt be saved. For with the heart man believeth unto righteousness and with the mouth, confession is made unto salvation." Romans 10:9-10

Just like the provision of salvation was made real in your life through faith in your heart (mind) and confession by your mouth, in the same vein, other redemptive work provisions will be made a reality in your life.

"For though we walk in the flesh, we do not war after the flesh: (for the weapons of our warfare are not carnal, but mighty through God to the pulling down of strongholds;) casting down imaginations, and every high thing that exalts itself against the knowledge of God, and bringing into captivity every thought to the obedience of Christ." II Corinthians 10:3-5

Arguably, this is where we lose our victory to the devil. The devil fills us up with symptoms, feelings, signs and facts, but he lies against the truth, which is the life of faith. In the school of faith, what is seen is temporary, while what is unseen is eternal. So, believing the unseen truth is the real fight of faith.

"In hope of eternal life, which God, that cannot lie, promised before the world began." Titus 1:2

"That by two immutable things, in which it was impossible for God to lie, we might have a strong consolation, who have fled for refuge to lay hold upon the hope set before us." Hebrews 6:18

To help boost your faith, I want to put it to you that God has never said a lie. He can never lie and will never lie. He is a God that has the power to do what He says, and whatever He says, He has already done. So, you must be determined to see it become a reality in your life.

---

*Faith is the agreement between
what is in your heart and what is
said with your mouth.*

Until then, nobody can have the reality of the promises of God in his or her life.

"Therefore, I say unto you, what things so ever ye desire, when ye pray, believe that ye receive them, and ye shall have them." Mark 11:24

"That the communication of thy faith may become effectual by the acknowledging of every good thing which is in you in Christ Jesus." Philemon 1:6

You don't win a battle until what is in your heart agrees with what is said with your mouth. In other words, wishing for or meditating on solutions doesn't win a battle - it must be communicated.

"We having the same spirit of faith, according as it is written, I believed and therefore have I spoken, we also believe and therefore speak." II Corinthian 4:13

Confession is the spirit of faith.

Anything you believe in and you do not confess regularly will soon become doubt in a matter of time.

Confession helps your faith to stay strong. So, the real template of what you believe is in your conversation. For out of the abundance of the heart, the mouth speaks, as said in Matthew 12:34.

This world was created by the Word, and it is being sustained by words (John1:1-3, Hebrews 1:3).

If the devil can defeat you in words,
then he has defeated you in real life.

Eve was defeated in the Garden of Eden via words, but thank God, Jesus defeated the devil via the Word in the wilderness.

The battle between Goliath and the Israelites was a battle of words. Goliath silenced the Israelites for forty days through words. Israel went into hiding. Words have a way of rendering your strength, weapon or tools impotent. Israel couldn't lift a finger. They had all the machinery of war, but they were already defeated through words.

Words empower and also incapacitate people. Help yourself by lifting your spirit via the Word of God. Doubt, fear, worries are all out there, but you can build your inward environment of certainty, peace and assurance through the Word of God.

"For the word of God is quick, and powerful and sharper than any two-edged sword, piercing even to the dividing asunder of soul and spirit, and of the joint and marrow, and is a discerner of the thought and intents of the heart. Neither is there any creature that is not manifest in his sight: but all things are naked and opened unto the eyes of him with whom we have to do. Seeing then that we have a great high priest, that

is passed into heaven, Jesus the son of God, let us hold fast our profession." Hebrews 4:12-14

"For by thy words thou shall be justified, and by thy words thou shall be condemned." Matthew 12:37

"And they overcame him by the blood of the lamb and by the words of their testimony, and they love not their lives unto death." Revelations 12:11

Confessing the testimony of what God has done through the redemptive work of Christ is what gives you victory in reality. David came to the scene of the battle where the armies of Israel had been silent for forty days and broke the silence by unmasking the Philistine, Goliath, through the weapon of words: 'Who is this uncircumcised Philistine?' Wow, what a revelation! David knew God made a covenant with Abraham and his seed through circumcision. So, the circumcision was the seal of God's ownership and warranty over Israel concerning all His promises to them among which is victory or deliverance in battle (I Samuel 17:24-26, 34-37, 45-51).

David understood the promise and was able to identify Goliath.

You need to understand
God's promise for
your life to fight the battle.

Furthermore, the story of the twelve spies sent into Canaan is another perfect example under this subject. Ten out of the twelve spies spoke what they saw. They described exactly what the environment painted to them and even concluded they were grasshoppers in their own sight. However, the remaining two spies; Joshua and Caleb stilled the people. They spoke from the perspective of what God had said. They created their view of the situation by the promise God made with them and confidently said they were able to possess the promised land (Numbers 13:26-33). And God said He would do according to what they have said in His ear (Numbers 14:28).

The latter end of the story was that only Joshua and Caleb entered the promised land out of the twelve spies because what they said affected them. Your mouth is a seal to what God can do for you. You negotiate your progress, victory, success via the words you speak.

---

*If the devil can withhold your
language, then he can withhold
your luggage.*

Every success you have recorded so far in your life is a measure of how you have fended with your words. It shows how far you have gone in this battle of faith.

---

*The victory you have not seen in your
life is because you lost your ground
in your heart and in your words.*

Stand therefore and see the salvation of the Lord. Stop losing it so soon in your heart and your words because of a little storm. Every word of God must be tested to show its validity.

Pray until your joy is full. Fight till victory is won (Luke 11:5-13).

CHAPTER FIVE
PRINCIPLES OF FASTING AND PRAYERS

1. Fasting is a platform for spiritual empowerment. To disarm your enemy, you need to be empowered.

Jesus prayed and fasted for 40 days, and He returned in the power of the Spirit (Luke 4:14). In other words, He returned empowered.

Prayer and fasting empower you into higher realms. You need to desire a higher realm of empowerment, during any prayer and fasting.

2. It is to have your enemies subdued. It takes being in power to have your enemies subdued. Psalms 66:3b says: "...through the greatness of thy power shall thine enemies submit themselves unto thee."

3. Fasting is ordained as a platform for the execution of vengeance. Execution of vengeance is one of the major ways of dealing with the wickedness of the wicked. Fasting is a platform for vengeance since the enemy won't go without vengeance (Ecclesiastes 8:11).

Jesus said: 'Howbeit this kind goeth not out but by prayer and fasting'(Matthew 17:21). Certain things have not been working out in your life, because the wicked are holding on to those areas. We cannot be wholly delivered from evil until the judgment is fully executed against the source.

4. Fasting provides a platform for accessing striking revelations. 'And ye shall know the truth, and the truth shall make you free' (John 8:32). Striking revelation connotes intense divine illumination, which guarantees your freedom from the powers of darkness (John 1:5; Isaiah 58:8).

Therefore, take advantage of the fasting season to access striking revelations that establish your dominion over the power of darkness.

---

*When you are fasting without
praying and searching God's Word,
you are on a hunger strike. Searching
through scriptures and praying is
what unleashes the real value of fasting.*

5.

---

*We can destroy the hold of
the devil through the weapons
of prayer and fasting.*

Jesus said: 'And from the days of John the Baptist until now the kingdom of heaven suffereth violence, and the violent take it by force' (Matthew 11:12). So, let's get spiritually violent against our tormentors, captors and the witches bewitching our destinies (Exodus 22:18).

6. Fasting enhances answers to prayers. "Then shalt thou call, and the Lord shall answer…" (Isaiah 58:9). Fasting is a spiritual booster for answered prayers. As you pray and fast, you will have express answers, in the precious name of Jesus Christ! Glory! Jesus is Lord!

The Power of Corporate Prayer

Why fast corporately?

1. With corporate fast comes corporate blessing. Esther fasted corporately with the children of Israel and received the reward of fasting (Esther 4:15-16). *"Then Esther bade them return Mordecai this answer: Go, gather together all the Jews that are present in Shushan, and fast ye for me; neither eat nor drink for three days, night or day. I also and my maidens will fast likewise, and so will I go in unto the king, which is not according to the law; and if I perish, I perish!"*

This was a crucial time for the Jews in Persia. By God's grace, Esther, a Jewess, had been chosen queen in place of Queen Vashti. It was also the time when Haman, the king's second-in-command, sought to destroy all the Jews in the entire kingdom because Mordecai, a Jew, did not bow down to him. He instigated King Ahasuerus to issue a decree to wipe out the Jews and was even willing to pay 10,000 talents of silver into the king's treasuries to finance the work. Refusing the silver, the king nevertheless agreed with Haman and gave him his signet ring to seal the decree (Esther 3:10, 12).

This was a very serious matter because even the king himself could not revoke any decree sealed with the king's signet ring. A death sentence thus hung over the Jews as they waited for the date set by their enemy to kill them.

Now her people were in great danger, and Mordecai was asking her to go to the king and beg for mercy on their behalf (Esther 5:3). So, it was when the king saw Queen Esther standing in the court that she found favour in his sight, and the king held out to Esther the golden sceptre that was in his hand. Then Esther went near and touched the top of the sceptre.

Corporate fast releases corporate favour. In the case of Israel, a whole generation was spared due to fasting.

There is power in agreement: "...if two of you agree on earth concerning anything that they ask, it will be done for them by my father in heaven" (Matthew 18:19, paraphrased).

2. Much bigger problems can be attacked and overcome when we fast together. An example to illustrate this is the church's prayer for Peter in Acts 4:23-37.

3. Fasting with others is a great source of encouragement.

4. The issues that we fast about corporately affect each of us individually. When we are fasting as a family, as a church, that will ultimately affect our individual lives. As long as we gather corporately, in one mind and spirit, the purpose in which we fast will inevitably also reflect positively in the lives of the part takers. Be it, finance, marriage, career, childbearing fruitfulness, etc. This is also true for the individuals who may not necessarily have issues, or presently have those things in their lives. Let us take finance or childbearing fruitfulness as examples. Someone who corporately joins a fast about the betterment of, say, church member's financial lives, this prayer will be effective, despite those who may be financially sound. Likewise, with childbearing, prayer is a seed that has its time for harvesting, according to God's perfect will.

5. Fasting together draws us together. As we go through fasting together, we will see our relationships strengthened as the Holy Spirit shows us our hearts and how we can better love and serve one another.

6. Fasting focuses all of us in the same direction. This entails, being focused centrally on God, His Word, His Spirit, His Will and His purposes for all.

Esther found favour before the King.

As we fast corporately, expect big favour before the King of kings and the Lord of lords upon your life, in your families, your place of work, your community and every sphere of your influence in Jesus' name.

Is there a problem in your life that seems unsolvable? FAST!

Is there an addiction that seems to be too hard to be broken? FAST!

Do you want to see the hand of God in that situation? FAST!

Do you desire a closer relationship with God the Father, God the Son and God the Holy Spirit? FAST!

In Matthew 6:16–18, Jesus also emphasised that the Father will reward fasting.

Some of the rewards are external, as God's power touches our circumstances. Some of our rewards are internal, as we encounter God with our hearts.

More importantly, we fast both to walk in more of God's power to change the world and to encounter more of His heart to change our heart! For God will give us the grace to fast, and if we ask for the grace to fast, we will receive it (II Peter 1:2; 3:18).

CHAPTER SIX
SET TIME FOR GLORY

*T**hou shall arise, and have mercy upon Zion: for the time to favour her, yea the set time is come.* Psalms 102:1

This book is not just to give you theoretical knowledge of what glory entails but to make you experience glory in its grand style. As a ministry, family, colleague or individual reading this book, I will give you the spiritual injunction to go on a journey of **21 days of fasting and prayer.** This is to hand over to you your prophetic inheritance called glory in any aspect you deem fit.

You can't pray and fast for 21 consecutive days without something happening.

The devil was not permitted to hinder Daniel's prayer beyond 21 days. Daniel was not only liberated, but his answer came also, and we never heard that his prayer was hindered again as the angel had given him the key to overcome the next demon that may afflict him (Daniel 10:1-21). That is why I know as you pray and fast, help will arise for you and delay or hindrance shall be a thing of the past. I decree that this will be a season of experiencing deeper intimacy with God in Jesus' name. May your strength be renewed like the eagle, and may every yoke that has denied you from manifesting the fullness of God's glory be broken in your life in Jesus' mighty name (Isaiah 40:31; 58:6).

The Bible says in Romans 8:19 *"for the earnest expectation of the creature waiteth for the manifestation of the sons of God."*

WHY ARE WE FASTING?

Value invites cost; nothing of high value is free.

You have to pay the price before you are allowed to carry the valuables.

The price you pay determines what you carry.

If you don't pay the price, you are not allowed to carry the goods (Proverbs 27:21).

Also, our blessings are first spiritual before they become physical (Ephesians 1:3), so you must pay the spiritual price so that you can receive the blessings. This fast is to help you align yourself to the frequency God is moving in your life.

Certain blessings will not come except by prayer and fasting (Matthew 17:20-21, Isaiah 58:6-8, Isaiah 30:18-19, Luke 4:1,14).

During this season, believers are encouraged to substitute times of eating with times of prayer, rely on the Word of God to transform your life. In doing so, it will allow Him to conform your will to His will. Know that fasting does not change God; fasting changes you!

During this fasting, give up things that would be a distraction for a while, including TV, DVDs, video games and social networking.

A word to couples: during this time, married couples should also abstain from intimate relationships (I Corinthians 7:3-5).

It is my prayer that you will show forth God's glory in every aspect of your life in Jesus' name.

I am looking forward to hearing your testimonies after and during these 21 days of fasting and prayer.

Glory awaits you.

DAY 1

Prayer Points

Instructions: Pray these points, along with your personal prayer focus list for the day. Feel free to add other scripture references as you pray.

Scriptures:

Psalms 96, Psalms 34:1-3, Psalms 24:6-10, Psalms 50:23, Psalms 84:11, Isaiah 40:5, Romans 3:23, John 11:4, Romans 8:19, 2Corinthians 3:18, Haggai 2:9, Isaiah 60:1.

1. Thank God for what He has already done for you and for that which He's doing and for what He will yet do in your life, your family and His church. (Psalms 96:3)

2. Thank God, for there shall be a manifestation of His glory in every area of your lives according to His Word. (Isaiah 40:5)

3. Glory be to God in the highest for His kingdom shall come; His power and glory shall be in manifestation in your life. (Psalms 57:5)

4. Father, we ask for mercy against anything the enemy has done, or we have done to cause us to fall short of God's glory in Jesus' name. (Romans 3:23)

5. Father, give me the power to live above sin and the activities of the flesh, that Your glory may be activated and revealed in my life in Jesus' name.

DAY 2

Prayer Points

Instructions: Pray these points, along with your personal prayer focus list for the day. Feel free to add other scripture references as you pray.

Scriptures:

Psalms 96, Psalms 34:1-3, Psalms 24:6-10, Psalms 50:23, Psalms 84:11, Isaiah 40:5, Romans 3:23, John 11:4, Romans 8:19, 2Corinthians 3:18, Haggai 2:9, Isaiah 60:1.

1. Lord, I decree upon my life, wife, husband, children, family, church and pastor the anointing to overtake and recover lost ground and glory. (Joel 2:25-27)

2. I decree His glory that brings peace into my home and family. May strife cease in my home from now on by the manifestation of His glory in Jesus' name. (John 17:22)

3. My God shall supply all my needs according to His riches in glory in the name of Jesus. (Philippians 4:19)

4. I decree and declare that the glory of God will bring me to prominence, where I will be recognised and rewarded in Jesus' name.

5. I decree the splendour, magnificence and the brilliance of God will be evident in our life, ministry and our nation in Jesus' name. (Ephesians 3:16)

DAY 3

Prayer Points

Instructions: Pray these points, along with your personal prayer focus list for the day. Feel free to add other scripture references as you pray.

Scriptures:

Psalms 96, Psalms 34:1-3, Psalms 24:6-10, Psalms 50:23, Psalms 84:11, Isaiah 40:5, Romans 3:23, John 11:4, Romans 8:19, 2Corinthians 3:18, Haggai 2:9, Isaiah 60:1.

1. Father, please bring me to my own glory. The glory You have prepared for me in this season, bring me into it, bring my children into it, bring my spouse, my family into the glory You have prepared for us in Jesus' name. (Hebrews 2:10)

2. I decree that youth and young adults will be drawn by God's Spirit to seek Him with all their hearts and that their lives shall glorify You. (Matthew 25:31)

3. To you, Lord, be all the glory for answers to prayers. (Isaiah 42:8)

4. I decree and declare that this is my season of His glory.

5. I am created and alive to show forth His glory!

DAY 4

Prayer Points

Instructions: Make these decrees along with your personal prayer focus list for the day. Feel free to add other scripture references as you pray.

Scriptures:

Psalms 96, Psalms 34:1-3, Psalms 24:6-10, Psalms 50:23, Psalms 84:11, Isaiah 40:5, Romans 3:23, John 11:4, Romans 8:19, 2Corinthians 3:18, Haggai 2:9, Isaiah 60:1.

Prophetic Declarations:

"You will also declare a thing, and it will be established for you; so light will shine on your ways." Job 22:2

1. I decree and declare that this is my season of His glory.

2. I am created and alive to show forth His glory!

3. I decree and declare that the King of Glory has come, and His glory shall be revealed mightily in my life!

4. His glory will be seen upon me!

5. God will get the glory out of my life!

DAY 5

Prayer Points

Instructions: Make these decrees along with your personal prayer focus list for the day. Feel free to add other scripture references as you pray.

Scriptures:

Psalms 96, Psalms 34:1-3, Psalms 24:6-10, Psalms 50:23, Psalms 84:11, Isaiah 40:5, Romans 3:23, John 11:4, Romans 8:19, 2Corinthians 3:18, Haggai 2:9, Isaiah 60:1.

1. Jesus the door; shut every evil door the enemy has opened in my life, marriage, finances, health, etc.

2. Father, direct me to my opened doors of blessings.

3. Jesus, You are the master door, in Your mercy open every great door that has closed before me now, in Jesus' name.

4. Father, as You open these doors, grant me the grace to walk through successfully.

5. I dislodge by fire every onslaught of the enemy at the gate of my life this year and the years beyond.

DAY 6

Prayer Points

Instructions: Make these decrees along with your personal prayer focus list for the day. Feel free to add other scripture references as you pray.

Scriptures:

Psalms 96, Psalms 34:1-3, Psalms 24:6-10, Psalms 50:23, Psalms 84:11, Isaiah 40:5, Romans 3:23, John 11:4, Romans 8:19, 2Corinthians 3:18, Haggai 2:9, Isaiah 60:1.

1. I possess the gate of my enemies this month and in the years ahead in Jesus' name. Amen!

2. Every gateman who is standing at the gate of a strong city, resisting my entry this month, hear the verdict of heaven: be paralysed and be disgraced by fire.

3. Lord, open wide the doors of heavenly blessings upon my life, family, ministry, etc.

4. I claim infinite open heavens over my life, marriage, family, etc.

5. Lord, spring open the flood gates of heaven and release an avalanche of blessings upon as angels ascend and descend unto me.

DAY 7

Prayer Points

Instructions: Make these decrees along with your personal prayer focus list for the day. Feel free to add other scripture references as you pray.

Scriptures:

Psalms 96, Psalms34:1-3, Psalms 24:6-10, Psalms 50:23, Psalms 84:11, Isaiah 40:5, Romans 3:23, John 11:4, Romans 8:19, 2Corinthians 3:18, Haggai 2:9, Isaiah 60:1.

1. I decree, declare, pronounce and proclaim that each closed door of favour by the devil, familiar spirits, witchcraft and marine spirits be open by Holy Ghost fire.

2. Lord, open wide all doors you have ordained for me and close all hell doors permanently in Jesus' name.

3. Lord, I ask that you restore all that I have lost as a result of ignorance, witchcraft and closed doors by the enemy.

4. Lord, open the gates of the spirit of life in Christ Jesus and set me free from the door of the shadows of death.

5. I shatter, scatter and set ablaze by the Holy Ghost fire every satanic door, brass door, cursed ancestral door, iron and limitation door, closed against my progress and my family.

DAY 8

Prayer Points

Instructions: Make these decrees along with your personal prayer focus list for the day. Feel free to add other Scripture references as you pray.

Scriptures:

Psalms 96, Psalms 34:1-3, Psalms 24:6-10, Psalms 50:23, Psalms 84:11, Isaiah 40:5, Romans 3:23, John 11:4, Romans 8:19, 2Corinthians 3:18, Haggai 2:9, Isaiah 60:1.

1. I thank God for His mercies over my life and His loving kindness.

2. Father, let my heavens be opened for divine open doors in Jesus' name.

3. Father, doors that no man can open, open them for me in Jesus' name.

4. Father, let my heaven be open for divine blessings in Jesus' name.

5. Father, let me enjoy open heavens throughout this year in Jesus' name.

DAY 9

Prayer Points

Instructions: Make these decrees along with your personal prayer focus list for the day. Feel free to add other Scripture references as you pray.

Scriptures:

Psalms 96, Psalms 34:1-3, Psalms 24:6-10, Psalms 50:23, Psalms 84:11, Isaiah 40:5, Romans 3:23, John 11:4, Romans 8:19, 2Corinthians 3:18, Haggai 2:9, Isaiah 60:1.

1. Father, let my door of promotion be open throughout this year in Jesus' name.

2. Father, let me enjoy academic open doors throughout this year in Jesus' name.

3. Father, let marital doors be open unto me this year in Jesus' name.

4. Father, wherever good doors have been shut upon me, let them be open in Jesus' name.

5. Father, let doors of good things be open unto me in Jesus' name.

DAY 10

Prayer Points

Instructions: Make these decrees along with your personal prayer focus list for the day. Feel free to add other scripture references as you pray.

Scriptures:

Psalms 96, Psalms 34:1-3, Psalms 24:6-10, Psalms 50:23, Psalms 84:11, Isaiah 40:5, Romans 3:23, John 11:4, Romans 8:19, 2Corinthians 3:18, Haggai 2:9, Isaiah 60:1.

1. Father, let doors of my progress be open unto me in Jesus' name.

2. Father, let doors of international connections be open to me in Jesus' name.

3. Father, throughout this year, may I operate under open heavens in Jesus' name.

4. Father, let the doors of my success be open onto me in Jesus' name.

5. Thank God for answered prayers.

DAY 11

Prayer Points

Instructions: Make these decrees along with your personal prayer focus list for the day. Feel free to add other scripture references as you pray.

Scriptures:

Psalms 96, Psalms 34:1-3, Psalms 24:6-10, Psalms 50:23, Psalms 84:11, Isaiah 40:5, Romans 3:23, John 11:4, Romans 8:19, 2Corinthians 3:18, Haggai 2:9, Isaiah 60:1.

1. This year, the Lord will put praises in my mouth. Every gate that is closing me in, whether they be gates of brass or bars of iron, the Lord will break them in pieces and set me free in Jesus' name. (Psalm 107:15-16, Isaiah 45:2)

2. Every prosperous gate of the New Year, I command your heads to be lifted up so that the King of Glory may enter with me to take over my possessions. I decree and declare every gate that has closed before now, begin to open in the mighty name of Jesus. (Psalms 24: 7)

3. Every gate in the New Year that will lead me to liberty begin to open of your own accord in Jesus' name. (Acts 12:10, Esther 5:2)

5. This year, O Lord, I open the doors of my heart; come and dine with me. Let not your presence depart from me. Be my companion at every moment. Let me enjoy your company the more this year. (Revelation 3:20)

Day 12

Prayer Points

Instructions: Make these decrees along with your personal prayer focus list for the day. Feel free to add other scripture references as you pray.

Scriptures:

Psalms 96, Psalms 34:1-3, Psalms 24:6-10, Psalms 50:23, Psalms 84:11, Isaiah 40:5, Romans 3:23, John11:4, Romans 8:19, 2Corinthians 3:18, Haggai 2:9, Isaiah 60:1.

1. This year, when it remains a little for the enemy to laugh over me, the Lord will show up for my release. (Acts 12: 6-7)

2. Lord, this new year, You will open unto me Your goodness to make me enter Your gates with thanksgiving. (Deut 28:12, Psalms 100:4) Begin to praise the Lord and worship Him for possessing the gates of your life.

3. In the name of Jesus Christ, I seal all back doors and windows that provide leakage and access to my enemies.

4. Lord, because of Your open doors of blessings over my life, bypass policies, protocols, politics, procedures, process and routines to favour me in Jesus' mighty name.

5. This year, the Lord will stir the hearts of men to pray for my release from every bondage. (Acts 12:5)

DAY 13

Prayer Points

Instructions: Make these decrees along with your personal prayer focus list for the day. Feel free to add other scripture references as you pray.

Scriptures:

Psalms 96, Psalms 34:1-3, Psalms 24:6-10, Psalms 50:23, Psalms 84:11, Isaiah 40:5, Romans 3:23, John 11:4, Romans 8:19, 2Corinthians 3:18, Haggai 2:9, Isaiah 60:1.

1. Every door that I will be knocking on this year and beyond, O Lord, let them open for me speedily. (Matthew 7:7)

2. Father, let doors of right contacts be opened unto me in Jesus' name.

3. Father, where others are struggling this year, Lord, let my heaven be opened this year in Jesus' name.

4. Father, let me enjoy financial open doors throughout this year in Jesus' name.

5. Lord, You have promised to restore my glory, my destiny, my fortune, my wasted years. Bring it to pass speedily. (Joel 2:23-25)

DAY 14

Prayer Points

Instructions: Make these decrees along with your personal prayer focus list for the day. Feel free to add other scripture references as you pray.

Scriptures:

Psalms 96, Psalms 34:1-3, Psalms 24:6-10, Psalms 50:23, Psalms 84:11, Isaiah 40:5, Romans 3:23, John 11:4, Romans 8:19, 2Corinthians 3:18, Haggai 2:9, Isaiah 60:1.

1. Anything covering my glory, preventing it from shining, burn by fire in Jesus' name. For it is written, "But we all, with unveiled face, beholding as in a mirror the glory of the Lord, are being transformed into the same image from glory to glory..." (II Corinthians 3:18) No weapon fashioned against my glory will prosper in Jesus' name.

2. In this season of His glory, Father God, show me Your glory in greater dimensions. Let Your glory be seen in our services and events in Jesus' name. (Exodus 33:18)

3. Father, clothe me with Your glory. Let the appearance of Your glory cause darkness to disappear in my life. (Isaiah 60:1)

4. I prophesy "they shall speak of the glory of God's kingdom, and talk of His power" in my life, in the name of Jesus. (Psalms 145:11)

5. Ancient doors of my father's house, be uprooted by fire in Jesus' name. Amen!

DAY 15

Prayer Points

Instructions: Make these decrees along with your personal prayer focus list for the day. Feel free to add other scripture references as you pray.

Scriptures:

Psalms 96, Psalms 34:1-3, Psalms 24:6-10, Psalms 50:23, Psalms 84:11, Isaiah 40:5, Romans 3:23, John 11:4, Romans 8:19, 2Corinthians 3:18, Haggai 2:9, Isaiah 60:1.

1. Oh my heavens over my head, open by fire.

2. I am the manifestation of God's glory, the embodiment of His goodness and the work of God's grace.

3. I am the carrier of His glory.

4. I decree and declare that the King of Glory has come and His glory shall be revealed mightily in my life!

5. His glory will be seen upon me!

DAY 16

Prayer Points

Instructions: Make these decrees along with your personal prayer focus list for the day. Feel free to add other scripture references as you pray.

Scriptures:

Psalms 96, Psalms 34:1-3, Psalms 24:6-10,
Psalms 50:23, Psalms 84:11, Isaiah 40:5,
Romans 3:23, John 11:4, Romans 8:19,
2Corinthians 3:18, Haggai 2:9, Isaiah 60:1.

1. Father, from now on my life shall be devoted for Your glory for I am created for Your glory. (Isaiah 43:7)

2. Let everything I do from now on bring glory to God the Father, Son and the Holy Spirit in Jesus' name. (I Corinthians 10:31)

3. Oh Father God, You are my glory and the lifter up of my head. In this season of glory, lift up my head in the name of Jesus. (Psalms 3:3)

4. Father, let your words concerning my life come to pass as I am observing this fasting and prayer. (Isaiah 65:24)

5. Lord, let there be a performance of what Your mouth has spoken about my life, family, work, etc. (Isaiah 40:5)

DAY 17

Prayer Points

Instructions: Make these decrees along with your personal prayer focus list for the day. Feel free to add other scripture references as you pray.

Scriptures:

Psalms 96, Psalms 34:1-3, Psalms 24:6-10, Psalms 50:23, Psalms 84:11, Isaiah 40:5, Romans 3:23, John 11:4, Romans 8:19, 2Corinthians 3:18, Haggai 2:9, Isaiah 60:1.

1. Lord, glorify me by Yourself with the glory You created me with. (John 17:5)

2. Father, show Your greater glory in my family this year in the name of Jesus. (Exodus 33:18)

3. Lord, make Your goodness pass before me this year, every month, every week, every day, every hour, every minute, every second. Let Your goodness be the order the day for this year. (Exodus 33:19)

4. Father, let this year be gracious, and be merciful unto me in every area of my life (Exodus 33:19).

5. Father, as You make me enjoy your goodness this year, hide me under Your rock and let Your protection be sure over my life and my family. (Exodus 33:22)

DAY 18

Prayer Points

Instructions: Make these decrees along with your personal prayer focus list for the day. Feel free to add other scripture references as you pray.

Scriptures:

Psalms 96, Psalms 34:1-3, Psalms 24:6-10,
Psalms 50:23, Psalms 84:11, Isaiah 40:5,
Romans 3:23, John 11:4, Romans 8:19,
2Corinthians 3:18, Haggai 2:9, Isaiah 60:1.

1. Father, by the blood of Jesus, we destroy the interference of the devil against the growth of my life, business and family in the name of Jesus. (Revelation 12:11)

2. Father, let my family, business and church experience supernatural growth from now on in the name of Jesus. (Ezekiel 36:37)

3. Father, envelope my glory (wife, husband, children, etc.) with Your fire that no devil will be able to touch us. (Exodus 24:17)

4. Lord, I must leave with glory as I tarried in Your presence in this fasting. I must not remain the same after this prayer. (I Chronicles 16:27)

5. Father, I must not be stripped of my glory; my crown must not be taken from my head. Protect me and my glory. (Job 19:9)

DAY 19

Prayer Points

Instructions: Make these decrees along with your personal prayer focus list for the day. Feel free to add other scripture references as you pray.

Scriptures:

Psalms 96, Psalms 34:1-3, Psalms 24:6-10, Psalms 50:23, Psalms 84:11, Isaiah 40:5, Romans 3:23, John 11:4, Romans 8:19, 2Corinthians 3:18, Haggai 2:9, Isaiah 60:1.

1. Father, let my glory sing praises this year, may it not be silent. (Psalms 30:12)

2. Father, this year guide me, lead me and teach me into glory. (Psalms 73:24)

3. Father, protect every seed that comes out of my loin. My crown must not fall off. (Proverbs 17:6)

4. Lord, protect me for my family, wife, husband and children. My glory must not wane. (Proverbs 17:6)

5. Lord, I must not be stroked with sickness. Build your wall around me. (Proverbs 20:29)

DAY 20

Prayer Points

Instructions: Make these decrees along with your personal prayer focus list for the day. Feel free to add other scripture references as you pray.

Scriptures:

Psalms 96, Psalms 34:1-3, Psalms 24:6-10, Psalms 50:23, Psalms 84:11, Isaiah 40:5, Romans 3:23, John 11:4, Romans 8:19, 2Corinthians 3:18, Haggai 2:9, Isaiah 60:1.

1. Father, I must not die with my glory. Protect me, protect my glory. (Isaiah 5:14)

2. Every member of my family, from the great to the least, shall all experience glory this year. Shame, failure, sickness, sorrow shall be far from us. (Isaiah 14:18)

3. Lord, this year, none of our investments, business, contract and work must collapse. (Isaiah 21:16)

4. This year, the glory of God shall judge every enemy that wants to rise up against me. (Isaiah 59:19)

5. Lord, as You glorify and bless me this year, let me remain humble; pride must not eat me up. (Jeremiah 9:23-24, 13:16)

DAY 21

Prayer Points

Instructions: Make these decrees along with your personal prayer focus list for the day. Feel free to add other scripture references as you pray.

Scriptures:

Psalms 96, Psalms 34:1-3, Psalms 24:6-10, Psalms 50:23, Psalms 84:11, Isaiah 40:5, Romans 3:23, John 11:4, Romans 8:19, 2Corinthians 3:18, Haggai 2:9, Isaiah 60:1.

1. Father, let your glory be an emblem over my life, my family and church. (Ezekiel 10:4)

2. Father, shake the nations of the earth, and let my desires be released. (Habakkuk 2:7)

3. Lord, let your word become flesh in my life this year, and make the beauty of my life be seen. (John 1:14)

4. This year, I shall walk in both celestial glory and terrestrial glory. (I Corinthians 15:40)

5. This year, I will experience both the glory of God and the glory of man. (I Corinthians 11:7)

May all your petitions be granted in Jesus Mighty Name. Amen!

I await your glorious testimony.

9 781916 175013